Learning to Live

Learning to Live

to

Live

*Basic Facts About Life
in the Family of God*

– Keith M. Bailey –

Christian Publications
CAMP HILL, PENNSYLVANIA

Christian Publications Inc
3825 Hartzdale Drive, Camp Hill, PA 17011

Faithful, biblical publishing since 1883

ISBN: 0-87509-709-X

© 1997 by Christian Publications, Inc.

All rights reserved
Printed in the United States of America

97 98 99 00 01   5 4 3 2 1

Unless otherwise indicated,
Scripture taken from the
HOLY BIBLE:
NEW INTERNATIONAL VERSION ®.
Copyright © 1973, 1978, 1984
by the International Bible Society.
Used by permission of
Zondervan Bible Publishers.

Contents

Introduction

Jesus said, ". . . do not worry about your life, what you will eat or drink; or about your body, what you will wear. Is not life more important than food, and the body more important than clothes?" (Matthew 6:25).

The gospel presents true life to those who believe on Christ as Savior. The human conception of life is measured in terms of material things, pleasures, privileges, prestige and power. Unregenerate men, not knowing they are dead in trespasses and sins, seek all these things. Sin can bring nothing but death. The problem of sin must be dealt with before any viable offer of life can be made. Christ died for our sins and rose from the dead. He is now prepared to give eternal life to the repentant sinner. When we receive

Christ we receive a new and wonderful quality of life. "He who has the Son has life; he who does not have the Son of God does not have life" (1 John 5:12).

Becoming a Christian is being born into the family of God. The born-again believer is alive in Christ. The life of the Lord Jesus Christ has been imparted by divine action. Our whole being is alive because our spiritual nature has been resurrected from the death of sin.

We now must learn to live. In our previous state the grip of spiritual death gave us a mind-set to sin. Now Christ begins imparting new life by altering out thoughts, actions, feelings and ambitions so they conform to Him. The Bible contains all the help needed for learning to live the new life. This course of study is an introduction to the basic facts about life in Christ. Careful study of the course, with your Bible, will help you experience abundant life in Christ.

Chapter 1

The Gift of Eternal Life

God gives salvation as a free gift to everyone who believes: "For the wages of sin is death but the gift of God is eternal life in Christ Jesus our Lord" (Romans 6:23). Now that you have received this gift, you are to enjoy its blessings.

Sin made you ashamed, troubled and sorry; you were a slave to its power. So you came to Christ for forgiveness of your sins. Christ died and shed His blood, making it possible for you to be forgiven of your sins and to be delivered from them. God's Word gives your heart that assurance: "In him we have redemption through his blood, the forgiveness of sins, in accordance with the riches of God's grace" (Ephesians 1:7). You no longer are guilty and condemned. The power that made you keep on sinning is broken.

Now God looks at you as if you had never sinned. Your sins have been blotted out, and God will not remember them against you again: "As far as the east is from the west, so far has he removed our transgressions from us" (Psalm 103:12). "Look, the Lamb of God, who takes away the sin of the world!" (John 1:29).

The Lord Jesus Christ not only put God's Holy Spirit into your heart at the time you received everlasting life, but He sent the Holy Spirit as the Comforter who comes alongside to help you.

Before Jesus ascended to heaven, He promised not to leave His followers as orphans. He said, "I will ask the Father, and he will give you another Counselor to be with you forever" (John 14:16). The Holy Spirit is a Person, a Teacher to help you to understand the Word of God and a Protector to guard your life against sin.

The Holy Spirit dwells in you and

checks your heart when you do something wrong. As you learn to obey Him, you will grow in the Lord.

It is important to be absolutely certain you are saved, and the Bible says you can know. How?

The answer is simple: God's Word is sure (1 John 5:13). The promises in the Bible are given so that you can know you have eternal life.

You also have the witness of the Holy Spirit in your heart to confirm that you are saved (Romans 8:16).

Memorize First John 5:11:

> *And this is the testimony: God has given us eternal life, and this life is in his Son.*

Answer these questions from the Bible:

Read the verses and think about their meaning. Then write down your answer. Do not copy the verses, but in your own words tell what they mean to you. Always depend on the Holy Spirit to give you understanding.

1. What assurance do you have that your sins are forgiven? 1 John 2:12

   _____
   _____
   _____

2. What has Jesus done for you by dying and shedding His blood?
   1 John 1:7; Revelation 1:5

   _____
   _____
   _____

3. What did you become when you believed and received the Lord Jesus Christ? John 1:12

   _____
   _____
   _____

4. Now that you are set free from the power of sin, whom are you to serve and obey as Master? What is the implication of Him being Master? Matthew 23:8

   _____
   _____
   _____

5. What has God provided to keep you from sinning and to help you to know how to live for Him? Psalm 119:11; Matthew 4:4

_____
_____
_____

6. What weapons must you use to overcome Satan? 1 John 2:14; Luke 22:40; 2 Corinthians 10:4-6

_____
_____
_____

7. How will the Holy Spirit help you? John 14:26

_____
_____
_____

Chapter 2

Your Spiritual Food

In order to live and keep your body well, it is necessary to eat good food every day. This law of nature has its counterpart in the Christian life. Just as your body needs food, your soul needs spiritual food each day. The Bible provides that food. Jesus said, "Man does not live on bread alone, but on every word that comes from the mouth of God" (Matthew 4:4).

The apostle Peter describes the food value of God's Word when he says, "Like newborn babies, crave pure spiritual milk, so that by it you may grow up in your salvation" (1 Peter 2:2). These words were written to new Christians. How fast you grow and how well you grow as a new believer depends on how you feed on the Word of God.

At the very beginning of your new life, form the habit of reading the Bible every day. You should decide what time of day is best for you and then set aside that time for this spiritual meal. Perhaps you may choose the morning as the best time, while your mind is fresh and free from cares of the day. Or you may prefer the evening when you are better able to relax and spend more time in the Word. This discipline is vitally important to learning the things of Christ.

Having a good plan for Bible reading is also important. Remember that all the Bible is God's Word, and reading the whole Book will contribute to your spiritual well-being. Some parts of the Bible are more difficult to understand than other parts. It is wise to begin with the simple passages of Scripture and progress to the more difficult. For your first Bible study, read the Gospel of Mark. Follow with the reading of the Gospel of John.

The following suggested plan will help you read the Bible with growing understanding:

1. After John's Gospel, read First John. This book is for Christians and gives important lessons about confessing sin, being sure of salvation and other subjects important for spiritual growth.

2. As your next study read the book of James, which tells you many practical things about the Christian life. Behavior and ethics are covered in this book.

3. The book of Romans gives a systematic study of the major doctrines of the Christian faith.

4. After reading the above books you will be prepared to begin with the Gospel of Matthew and read the entire New Testament.

5. At this point begin reading the Old Testament. The books of Psalms and Proverbs are a good starting place.

6. As soon as possible read the whole Bible through. Make it a lifetime habit to read and read and read your Bible.

Memorize Psalm 119:11:

I have hidden your word in my heart that I might not sin against you.

Answer these questions from the Bible:

1. How should you study the Bible?
   2 Timothy 2:15

   _____
   _____
   _____

2. How does God's Word help you?
   Psalm 119:105

   _____
   _____
   _____

3. How does memorizing God's Word help you? Psalm 119:11

   _____
   _____
   _____
   _____

4. What are you to do with what you have read? James 1:22, 25

_____
_____
_____

5. What happens if you don't put your faith in the Bible? Hebrews 4:2

_____
_____

6. What role does God's Word play in defending you from Satan's attacks? Ephesians 6:17

_____
_____
_____

7. Why should you read all of the Bible? 2 Timothy 3:16-17

_____
_____
_____

8. Where did the Bible come from? What kind of men wrote it? 2 Peter 1:21

_____
_____
_____

9. How long will God's Word last?
   1 Peter 1:25; Matthew 24:35

   _____
   _____
   _____

10. How does the Bible show you the
    condition of your heart? Hebrews
    4:12

    _____
    _____
    _____

Chapter 3

Talking with God

Your body cannot live without food. Neither can it live without air to breathe. Prayer is the breathing of your new life in Christ. Jesus said that believers ought to pray about everything so they will not become discouraged.

Praying is talking with God. It is necessary to be near to God in order to talk with Him. You cannot talk with someone who is far away and cannot hear you. When Christ saved you He brought you near to God. He opened heaven so you could talk with God the Father directly. You are invited to draw near to God (James 4:8).

The most enjoyable talks with God are the talks you have alone with Him, when no one else is with you. What should you talk with God about?

First of all, praise and thank Him for what He has done for you. Then tell God about your faults, weaknesses and sins, and ask the Lord to help you to be strong. Tell Him all your troubles and ask Him to guide you in your actions.

When you are worried and burdened about your loved ones and friends who have needs, tell God about them as you pray. Pray especially for those who need Christ. The heavenly Father is your Friend now, and He will be happy to listen to everything that is in your heart.

When it is possible, pray with other believers. Pray every day with those in your home. Gather your family together and let each one who believes pray. When other Christians visit your home, have prayer together before they leave. Meet often with other Christians for prayer.

Take time to pray. Christians learn to pray by praying.

Memorize Mark 11:24:

> *Therefore I tell you, whatever you ask for in prayer, believe that you have received it, and it will be yours.*

Answer these questions from the Bible:

1. Who gives you the right to pray to God? Whose name should you use? John 14:13-14; 16:23-24

   _____
   _____
   _____

2. To what kind of people does God give the privilege of prayer? 1 John 3:22; James 5:16

   _____
   _____
   _____

3. What will happen if you pray and still have a desire to sin in your heart? Psalm 66:18

   _____
   _____
   _____
   _____

4. What does Matthew 21:22 tell you
   God expects from you if He is to answer your prayer?

   _____
   _____
   _____
   _____

5. How do you know God will answer
   your prayer if you can't see how it
   will happen? Jeremiah 33:3; 1 John
   5:14-15

   _____
   _____
   _____
   _____

6. How will praying keep you from
   worry? Philippians 4:6-7

   _____
   _____
   _____

7. Who is your Helper when you pray?
   How does He help you? Romans
   8:26

   _____
   _____
   _____

8. What is the key to our confidence in approaching God? What is the result? 1 John 5:14-15

_____

_____

_____

9. What does God promise to those who pray together? Matthew 18:19-20

_____

_____

_____

Chapter 4

A New Person

When you became a Christian you began a whole new life. A person living in sin is dead toward God. When one receives Christ he or she is truly made alive.

Bad habits, sinful pleasures, unclean thoughts and desires must be put away from the Christian. Paul says, "Therefore, if anyone is in Christ, he is a new creation; the old has gone, the new has come!" (2 Corinthians 5:17).

Ask the Holy Spirit to show you those things in your life belonging to the old life which must go. Give them up right away, and the Lord will make you strong.

Your mind now belongs to the Lord. Ask Him to make your thoughts clean. Be careful to fill your mind with good thoughts. Read only those things that will help you keep a clean mind.

The Bible teaches that a Christian's body is the temple of the Holy Spirit—a holy place where God's Spirit lives. Any habit that harms the body, then, is sinful. Keep your body clean and pure. Use your body for the Lord.

Satan will tempt you. He will use even your friends and loved ones. You are now a child of God. Make up your mind that you will not walk into Satan's trap.

Use wisdom in the way you spend your leisure time. Choose friends who will strengthen you spiritually. Decide that you will forsake the ways and thoughts of the old life in favor of the ways and the thoughts of the new life in Christ.

Beginning your new life with definite separation from the world, the flesh and the devil will bring you inner peace and give credibility to your testimony.

Memorize Second Corinthians 5:17:

> *Therefore, if anyone is in Christ, he is a new creation; the old has gone, the new has come!*

Answer these questions from the Bible:

1. What are some specific sins that should not be in the lives of Christians? Galatians 5:19-21; Ephesians 4:25, 28, 31; 5:3

   _____
   _____
   _____
   _____
   _____
   _____

2. How should a Christian look at drinking? Proverbs 20:1

   _____
   _____
   _____

3. What does Second Corinthians 6:17-18 say about unclean things? How do Christians avoid them? Can you think of any unclean ar-

eas in your life you need to deal
with?

_____

_____

_____

_____

4. What kinds of things should you
   think about to keep your mind
   clean? Philippians 4:8

_____

_____

_____

_____

5. What should you ask God to do
   about your thoughts? Psalm
   139:23-24

_____

_____

_____

6. How does Christ feel about iniq-
   uity or sin? Hebrews 1:9

_____

_____

_____

_____

7. What do Romans 6:1-2, 12, 14 say about sinning as a Christian?

_____

_____

_____

_____

8. If you find out you have sinned, what should you do right away? What will God do? 1 John 1:9

_____

_____

_____

_____

Chapter 5

The Spirit-filled Life

The Holy Spirit comes to each believer to make him or her alive in Christ. The Spirit gives life and He sustains spiritual life daily. Christians are to have the Holy Spirit not only as Lifegiver, but they are to be filled with the Spirit.

The new believer may question, "How can I be filled with the Spirit?" To be filled with the Spirit is every believer's privilege. The Scriptures give the following conditions for being filled with the Holy Spirit. The first condition is consecrating oneself to God: "Therefore, I urge you, brothers, in view of God's mercy, to offer your bodies as living sacrifices, holy and pleasing to God—this is your spiritual act of worship." (Romans 12:1). The second condition is being willing to forsake all known sin and having a desire to be pure in heart (Acts 15:9). The third condition is having an attitude of ready obedience to the known will of God (Acts 5:32). The Scripture says, "Blessed are those who hunger and thirst for righteousness, for they will be filled" (Matthew 5:6). Jesus is teaching in this passage the value of spiritual desire. It is a necessary attitude for being filled with the Spirit.

When the believer understands, according to the Scriptures, the provision of the filling of the Spirit and has prepared his or her heart by meeting the above-mentioned conditions he is ready to pray. Jesus said, "If you then, though you are evil, know how to give good gifts to your children, how much more will your Father in heaven give the Holy Spirit to those who ask him!" (Luke 11:13). The believer comes to the Father in faith and simply asks that he or she be filled with the Spirit.

Jesus pictures the Spirit-filled life as a

river of living water overflowing with blessing: "On the last and greatest day of the Feast, Jesus stood and said in a loud voice, 'If anyone is thirsty, let him come to me and drink. Whoever believes in me, as the Scripture has said, streams of living water will flow from within him'" (John 7:37-38). The fullness of the Spirit brings abundance, completeness, power and victory.

The Holy Spirit not only fills the heart but He sanctifies the whole spirit, soul and body of the believer. The word *sanctify* means to separate from sin and dedicate to God for His holy purpose. God's purpose, according to the Scriptures, is to make the believer Christlike. After the Christian is filled with the Spirit and wholly sanctified, the growth process is accelerated. Being filled with the Spirit is not an end in itself but the introduction of an ongoing growth and development of holy living. Maturity comes by a process of growth in the grace and the knowledge of the Lord Jesus Christ. It is futile to seek such growth apart from total consecration and the filling of the Holy Spirit.

The believer is not able to overcome weakness and sin in his or her own strength. The life of victory is assured by Christ living in the believer. Victorious living is made possible through the Holy Spirit, Christ's personal representative to each individual Christian. It is by the Holy Spirit that Christ lives in you.

Memorize Ephesians 5:18:

> *Do not get drunk on wine, which leads to debauchery. Instead, be filled with the Spirit.*

Answer these questions from the Bible:

1. Who is the Holy Spirit? John 14:26; 16:13-14

   _____

   _____

   _____

2. What is the first ministry of the Holy Spirit? John 16:8

   _____

   _____

   _____

3. What is the Holy Spirit's work in the new birth? John 3:5; Titus 3:5

_____

_____

_____

4. Who sanctifies the believer? What does it mean to be santified? 1 Peter 1:2

_____

_____

_____

5. How does the Holy Spirit give power to the Christian? Ephesians 3:16-17

_____

_____

_____

6. In what ways is your life changed by the Holy Spirit when you become a Christian? Romans 8:3-6

_____

_____

_____

Chapter 6

Overcoming Temptation

It is only after becoming a Christian
that you understand what temptation
really is. After you have passed from the
darkness of spiritual death to the light of
eternal life in Christ you have virtually
changed masters. Before salvation you
served the devil; after salvation you serve
Christ. The devil does not abandon his
prey easily. He makes every subtle effort
to turn the believer away from following
Christ. The devil will deliberately try to
entice the Christian to sin. Even the Lord
Jesus Christ was tempted by the devil
during His earthly life.

All Christians experience temptation

in many forms. Sometimes the devil uses another person to tempt you or he may place an evil thought in your mind. Books, pictures, television, radio or any form of media may suggest wickedness— and even seek to make that wickedness look desirable.

God understands your battles with temptation and He has provided in His grace all the help you need to overcome temptation. Peter says that the devil goes about like a roaring lion. He does this to frighten the Christian and to make him or her feel helpless in the face of temptation. But the Word of God teaches that "the one who is in you is greater than the one who is in the world" (1 John 4:4). This means simply that Christ living in you is much stronger than the devil who is in the world.

Ask the Lord for His help and wisdom in overcoming temptation. Use the method Jesus used when He was tempted by the devil in the wilderness— He countered every suggestion of the devil with a Scripture passage. A good knowledge of the Bible will equip you to meet temptation.

Twice in the New Testament Christians are told to resist the devil.

"Resist him, standing firm in the faith" (1 Peter 5:9).

"Resist the devil, and he will flee from you" (James 4:7).

To resist the devil you must use your will. When you realize that the devil is trying to tempt you, immediately determine in your will to walk in God's way and not give in to the devil. By making that choice you will become stronger and will be able to overcome the temptation.

The crisis of temptation calls for the exercise of faith. The struggle with the tempter makes Christians aware of their many weaknesses and sends them to Christ for divine help. Paul called this spiritual action putting on the whole armor of God. As a soldier going into battle covers his vulnerable body with a metal armor, so the children of God in their battle with temptation need the covering of God's armor. At the cross Jesus won over the devil and crushed his power. This same victorious Christ will stand by your side in the hour of temptation and give you His strength. Revelation 12:11

says that the believers overcame Satan by the blood of the Lamb. Trust in the power of the blood and the devil will flee.

Memorize First Corinthians 10:13:

> *No temptation has seized you except what is common to man. And God is faithful; he will not let you be tempted beyond what you can bear. But when you are tempted, he will also provide a way out so that you can stand up under it.*

Answer these questions from the Bible:

1. How does God help the believer when he or she is tempted to sin? 1 Corinthians 10:13

   _____
   _____
   _____

2. What areas of your life will the enemy use to tempt you? 1 John 2:16

   _____
   _____
   _____
   _____

3. At what point can temptation become sin? James 1:13-15

_____

_____

_____

4. Make a list of the strategies of the devil to tempt the Christian.
2 Corinthians 4:3-4; 1 Peter 5:8-9

_____

_____

5. Why should the believer understand the possible ways the devil may use to tempt him or her? 2 Corinthians 2:10-11

_____

_____

_____

6. What are the weapons of the Christian for this spiritual war with the devil? 2 Corinthians 10:3-6; Ephesians 6:10-18

_____

_____

_____

Chapter 7

Facing Up to Persecution

Life in Christ is realistic. Christ lived in our real world, so He is a sufficient Savior for all people. The Christian life works because it faces the tensions of living in an alien world. Unsaved people are not friends of God's goodness and righteousness. They do not understand people who regulate their lives by the will of God. New Christians should be aware of the pressure that may come upon them as a result of their stand for Christ. The Scriptures call this persecution.

Christ prepared His disciples for this reality:

Blessed are those who are persecuted because of righteousness, for theirs is the kingdom of heaven.

Blessed are you when people insult you, persecute you and falsely say all kinds of evil against you because of me. Rejoice and be glad, because great is your reward in heaven, for in the same way they persecuted the prophets who were before you. (Matthew 5:10-12)

Jesus Christ did not advocate a fatalistic acceptance of the pressures and even sufferings which come to His people as a result of persecution. The Sermon on the Mount lays down a basic spiritual principle for dealing with persecution. Every Christian needs to understand that principle. Christ says that believers are persecuted because of their identification with Him. He also teaches in this passage that a proper reaction to persecution has its rewards both in this life and in the life to come.

The biggest battle a new believer faces is reacting wrongly to persecution from loved ones and friends. This persecution may take more than one form. Sometimes it is ridicule, or it may be disgust or even hate. How should a Christian act when treated this way by family members and associates? Jesus said to bless those who misuse you. Do not retaliate. The spirit of Christ is one of meekness and He calls His disciples to react in the same spirit.

First Peter 4:12-16 says,

> *Dear friends, do not be surprised at the painful trial you are suffering, as though something strange were happening to you. But rejoice that you participate in the sufferings of Christ, so that you may be overjoyed when his glory is revealed. If you are insulted because of the name of Christ, you are blessed, for the Spirit of glory and of God rests on you. If you suffer, it should not be as a murderer or thief or any other kind of criminal, or even as a meddler. However, if you suffer as a Christian, do not be ashamed, but praise God that you bear that name.*

It is a privilege to suffer for Christ. Suffering resulting from the believer's own mistakes and inconsistent living can only be changed by repentance. But suffering resulting from the believer's choice to do God's will wholeheartedly is attended with deep inner peace and blessing. The Holy Spirit enables the yielded believer to respond to suffering with praise rather than self-pity. In the providential working of God's Spirit, often the gracious spirit of the sufferer will ultimately win the persecutor to Christ. The Christian ought not to look for trouble, but when it comes he should realize the abundance of grace to help bear it. The Christlike practice of forgiving those who misuse you makes your Christian witness credible.

Memorize Second Timothy 2:12:

> *If we endure, we will also reign with him. If we disown him, he will also disown us.*

Answer these questions from the Bible:

1. Why does God permit believers to suffer for their faith? Romans 8:17; Philippians 3:10; Colossians 1:24

_____
_____
_____
_____

2. What are the rewards of suffering for Christ? Romans 8:18; 2 Timothy 2:12

_____
_____
_____
_____

3. What comfort is offered to the Christian in times of persecution and suffering? 2 Timothy 4:16-18; John 16:33

_____
_____
_____

4. What should Christians do while they are suffering? 1 Peter 4:19

_____
_____
_____

5. In what ways can suffering help to mature the believer? Romans 5:3-5

_____

_____

_____

6. What does suffering enable the child of God to do? How? 2 Corinthians 1:3-7

_____

_____

_____

Chapter 8

The Lord for the Body

The Lord Jesus Christ is a complete Savior. He purchased with His precious blood a redemption that includes the sinner's every need. It overcomes the results of sin and assures eternal life. The body of the Christian is included in redemption. Biblical salvation not only brings peace and spiritual blessing to the inner person, it includes the outer person as well. Salvation is for the whole person: spirit, soul and body.

The body is the temple of the Holy Spirit (1 Corinthians 6:19). The body is a member of Christ and therefore should be treated with reverence. The body is sanctified by Christ (1 Thessalonians 5:23). The body will be resurrected from the dead (1 Corinthians 15:20-23).

Health and healing are among the provisions of Christ for the Christian's body. Paul said, "The body is not meant for sexual immorality, but for the Lord, and the Lord for the body" (1 Corinthians 6:13). A wonderful new relationship is offered every Christian in this verse. As you present your body to Christ you may trust Christ for your bodily needs. The Lord Jesus Christ is Healer as well as Savior and Sanctifier.

The joy of the Christian life promotes good physical and mental health. But when the pressures of life bring illness on a child of God he or she may go to the Lord for healing. James instructs the Christian as to the procedure for asking healing of the Lord:

> *Is any one of you in trouble? He should pray. Is anyone happy? Let him sing songs of praise. Is any one of you sick? He should call the elders of the church to pray over him and anoint him with oil in the name of*

the Lord. And the prayer offered in faith will make the sick person well; the Lord will raise him up. If he has sinned, he will be forgiven. Therefore confess your sins to each other and pray for each other so that you may be healed. The prayer of a righteous man is powerful and effective." (James 5:13-16)

Memorize First Corinthians 6:13:

"Food for the stomach and the stomach for food"—but God will destroy them both. The body is not meant for sexual immorality, but for the Lord, and the Lord for the body.

Answer these questions from the Bible:

1. What is the basic cause of sickness in the human family? John 5:5-14

_____

_____

_____

_____

_____

2. What specific promises can be found in these passages? Exodus 15:26; Psalm 103:1-3

_____
_____
_____
_____

3. What do these verses say about healing today? Luke 9:1; Mark 16:18; James 5:13-16

_____
_____
_____
_____

4. What is the role of the Holy Spirit in physical healing? Romans 8:11

_____
_____
_____

5. What did Christ do to provide healing for His children? Isaiah 53:5; Matthew 8:17

_____
_____
_____
_____

6. What is the place of prayer in the ministry of healing? Acts 4:29-30; James 5:13-16

_____
_____
_____

Chapter 9

Witnessing for Christ

The personal witness of believers is God's method for reaching other people. Witnessing is confessing that Jesus Christ is your Savior, expressing your personal faith in Him.

Everyone should hear the good news of the gospel. The best way for others to hear about Christ is for you to tell them. Paul tells us that just as we believe in our heart we must also confess with our mouth that we have a personal faith in Christ as our Savior:

That if you confess with your mouth, "Jesus is Lord," and believe in your

*heart that God raised him from the
dead, you will be saved. For it is with
your heart that you believe and are
justified, and it is with your mouth
that you confess and are saved.* (Romans 10:9-10)

Telling others is an important part of
starting your life with Christ and of living this new life from day to day. Peter
said believers must always be ready to
tell those who ask the reason for their
trust in Christ: "But in your hearts set
apart Christ as Lord. Always be prepared
to give an answer to everyone who asks
you to give the reason for the hope that
you have" (1 Peter 3:15).

Jesus wants to use you in winning others to Himself. Start telling your family
and friends today about the new peace
you have in Christ. Pray about bringing
others to Jesus. Ask the Holy Spirit to
give you the power to speak the right
words at the right time. He will guide
you to people hungry for the gospel.

Every time you have opportunity to
speak for Christ, do it. Faithfulness in
witnessing strengthens your faith and

gives great joy. As you read your Bible, mark the verses that will help you explain the plan of salvation to others. Get a supply of gospel tracts and be prepared to use them as tools in expressing your faith.

Memorize Proverbs 11:30:

> *"The fruit of the righteous is a tree of life, and he who wins souls is wise."*

Answer these questions from the Bible:

1. What does the Bible say about a person who wins souls and brings people to God? Proverbs 11:30

_____

_____

_____

_____

2. What condition must we meet and how are we made "fishers of men"? Matthew 4:18-19

_____

_____

_____

_____

3. To what is the Christian asked to bear witness? Acts 2:32

_____
_____
_____
_____

4. What did Andrew and Philip do after they found Christ as their Savior? John 1:40-46

_____
_____
_____
_____
_____

5. How can you show God to others? Matthew 5:16

_____
_____
_____
_____

6. What is the reward in Daniel 12:3 for?

_____
_____
_____
_____

7. Jesus said that bringing others to Him is like harvesting a crop. When is the harvest ready? How can you help bring in the harvest? John 4:35

_____
_____
_____
_____

8. What is worth more than your soul? Mark 8:36-37

_____
_____
_____

9. What are we instructed to do? How can you carry this out? 1 Peter 3:15

_____
_____
_____

10. Think about Mark 16:15 and Luke 14:23. Where does Jesus ask you to go with the gospel? What sacrifices might this require?

_____
_____
_____

Chapter 10

Giving to God

God's Word says, "It is more blessed to give than to receive" (Acts 20:35). Sin makes one selfish. God gives the Christian a new mind so that he or she wants to give. Believers willingly give their life, strength, time, money and whatever they own to the Lord.

God owns everything, and you are just using what really belongs to Him. God is happy to give you whatever you need. Because of all that Christ has done for you, it should be easy for you to give back to Him whatever He may ask.

The Bible teaches the believer to tithe.

This means he or she should give to God at least ten percent of everything earned (Malachi 3:10).

If every Christian would obey God by tithing, there would always be enough money for God's work. Start now to tithe. Obedience to God will bring rich blessings from the Lord.

The believer's love for God motivates him to give to God. That which is given above the tithe is a love offering to God.

You must manage your money well in order to give as you should. Some Christians rob themselves of the joy of giving because they have made poor commitments of their money, so they have nothing to give God.

Money is a necessary means of exchange in our modern world and Scripture recognizes this reality. The Bible also recognizes the menace that money can be in the life of a believer. The sin of covetousness is deadly, twisting the personality so that the person in its grip lives to accumulate money.

The Word of God teaches the believer how to use his or her money for the glory of God. Money management for the

Christian is not just for the purpose of giving but because it represents a lifestyle compatible with divine standards.

Memorize Second Corinthians 9:7:

> *Each man should give what he has decided in his heart to give, not reluctantly or under compulsion, for God loves a cheerful giver.*

Answer these questions from the Bible:

1. What should be your motives for giving? 2 Corinthians 9:7

   _____
   _____
   _____
   _____

2. What does God promise if you obediently tithe? Malachi 3:10

   _____
   _____
   _____
   _____

3. God's Word says giving is like planting seeds because later you get back

more than you planted. What will happen if you don't give? 2 Corinthians 9:6

_____

_____

_____

4. On what day of the week should Christians bring their gifts for God to church? 1 Corinthians 16:2

_____

_____

5. Read Matthew 6:19-21. What are your "treasures"? How do you know whether or not they're the right kind, stored in the right place?

_____

_____

_____

6. Read the story in Mark 12:41-44. Why do you think Jesus was so pleased with what this woman did?

_____

_____

_____

7. Read Second Corinthians 8:9. What kind of example did Jesus give us by what He did for us?

_____

_____

_____

8. What does Psalm 41:1-3 say about the poor? What benefits are involved?

_____

_____

_____

9. What does Romans 10:14-15 ask us to do for people who are not saved?

_____

_____

_____

Chapter 11

A Church Home

The Lord Jesus Christ established His church as the spiritual home of believers. His church includes all true believers—of the past and of the present. When you believed on Christ as your Savior, you were baptized by the Spirit into Christ's body, the Church.

The Church is both visible and invisible—part of the whole Church being scattered throughout the world and part having already gone to be with the Lord in heaven. Christians must have more than a spiritual connection with the Church; they must identify themselves with the visible Church by becoming members of it.

A Christian needs fellowship with other believers. That fellowship may be found in a Bible-believing church which provides preaching, teaching and prayer. Meeting together with other Christians will help to strengthen your faith in the Lord Jesus Christ.

Jesus authorized the church to administer two ordinances for the spiritual good of His people—water baptism and the communion meal. You need the church because only there can you partake of these ordinances commanded by Christ.

Water baptism pictures the steps of salvation. As the repentant believer is immersed in the water, it symbolizes his or her identification with Christ in His death and burial. The baptismal candidate is saying to the world, "I stand with Christ and I believe His blood washes my sins away." As the believer is raised from the water the resurrection is in view. He or she is now raised to walk in newness of life through the power of the indwelling Christ (Romans 6:3-4).

Christ instituted communion as a reminder of His death for us and as a reminder that He is coming again. Communion is a term of fellowship when believers break bread (symbolizing Christ's body) together and drink the cup (symbolizing Christ's blood), remembering they have been made one by the death and resurrection of Christ.

Since being baptized and becoming a member of the church is so important, ask your counselor or the pastor about enrolling in the membership class in order to prepare yourself for this step of spiritual progress.

Memorize Matthew 18:20:

> *For where two or three come together in my name, there am I with them.*

Answer these questions from the Bible:

1. Who started the church? Matthew 16:16-18

   _____
   _____
   _____
   _____

2. Who is the leader or the "head" of the church? Ephesians 1:20-23

_____

_____

_____

_____

3. What requirement for church membership is given in this verse? Acts 2:47

_____

_____

_____

_____

4. Why is it important to attend church regularly? Hebrews 10:25

_____

_____

_____

_____

5. What spiritual steps come before water baptism? Acts 2:38; Mark 16:16

_____

_____

_____

_____

6. What is the purpose of communion?
   1 Corinthians 11:23-26

   _____

   _____

   _____

7. What happens when Christians meet
   in Christ's name? Matthew 18:20

   _____

   _____

   _____

Chapter 12

The Blessed Hope

The night before Jesus went to the cross He met in an upper room with His disciples. He told them a wonderful secret. Though God's plan of salvation required that Christ die on the cross, be buried, be raised from the dead and then return to the Father in heaven, there was still another step in this great plan: Jesus promised His disciples He would personally come back again (John 14:3). Christ's second coming will occur in two phases. The first phase of this great event will be to gather all true believers to Himself.

Paul tells exactly how this will take place:

*Brothers, we do not want you to be ig-
norant about those who fall asleep, or
to grieve like the rest of men, who
have no hope. We believe that Jesus
died and rose again and so we believe
that God will bring with Jesus those
who have fallen asleep in him. According to the Lord's own word, we tell
you that we who are still alive, who
are left till the coming of the Lord,
will certainly not precede those who
have fallen asleep. For the Lord himself will come down from heaven, with
a loud command, with the voice of the
archangel and with the trumpet call of
God, and the dead in Christ will rise
first. After that, we who are still alive
and are left will be caught up together
with them in the clouds to meet the
Lord in the air. And so we will be
with the Lord forever. Therefore en-
courage each other with these words.*
(1 Thessalonians 4:13-18)

For Christians who are alive when Jesus comes, an instantaneous change will
occur in their bodies. The perishable
mortal body will changed to a body like

Christ's beyond the reach of death. At the time of Christ's return, the body of the dead believer will be resurrected and shall be caught up to meet Christ in the air. Paul spoke of Christ's coming for His own as the "blessed hope." The coming of Christ for His church is imminent. Jesus taught His disciples to live in constant readiness for the Lord's return.

The second coming of Christ is not only the believer's personal hope and answer to the future; it is also his or her key to understanding the world in which he or she lives. Christ gave insight into the signs at the end of the age and of His second coming. Jesus taught that wickedness would continue to worsen in the world system and that demonic activity would be intensified. The apostle Paul described the last days as dangerous because of social unrest, violence and evil. Political systems will be devastated. Finally, in the dark hours of the tribulation (a period of judgment Christ has designed to deal with the nations of the world), Satan will bring forth his masterpiece, a world ruler called the antichrist. This diabolic leader will bring the wickedness of the nations to its highest level.

Then the Lord Jesus will return to the earth with His saints to establish His kingdom. Then Satan will be bound and the righteous government of Christ will prevail among all the nations of the world. The true believers will reign with Christ during the thousand years His kingdom will be on earth. At the end of the 1,000-year reign the earth will be judged with fire. Christ will then judge the wicked from His great white throne. After these events the new heavens and the new earth will begin. The saints will dwell in the city of God and enjoy the blessings of Christ's everlasting kingdom.

Memorize John 14:3:

And if I go and prepare a place for you, I will come back and take you to be with me that you also may be where I am.

Answer these questions from the Bible:

1. What present world conditions can you find described by Jesus in Matthew chapter 24?

   _____

   _____

2. Why did Paul refer to the second coming of Christ as "the blessed hope"? Titus 2:11-14

   _____

   _____

   _____

3. Where will Christ meet His people at the second coming? 1 Thessalonians 4:16-17

   _____

   _____

   _____

4. What will take place in the believer when he or she is caught up to meet the Lord? 1 Thessalonians 4:17; 1 Corinthians 15:50-54; Philippians 3:20-21

   _____

   _____

   _____

5. How may the believer prepare for the Lord's coming? 1 John 3:1-3; 1 Peter 4:7-10; 2 Peter 3:11, 14

_____

_____

_____

6. What is the responsibility of the Church until Christ returns? Matthew 28:19-20; Acts 1:8

_____

_____

_____

7. In the last days before Christ's coming what kinds of false religions will appear? 1 Timothy 4:1-5

_____

_____

_____

_____

8. How many resurrections do you find in the following Scripture? 1 Corinthians 15:20-24; Revelation 20:4-6

_____

_____

_____

9. By what will all people be judged?
   Revelation 20:11-15

   _____
   _____
   _____
   _____

10. List the characteristics of Christ's
    kingdom on earth after His return.
    Matthew 25:34; Isaiah 35; Zechariah
    14:4-11; Isaiah 2:1-5; Revelation
    19:11-16; 20:1-4

    _____
    _____
    _____
    _____
    _____
    _____
    _____
    _____

Other Books by
Keith M. Bailey

Care of Converts
The Children's Bread
Christ's Coming and His Kingdom
Servants in Charge